Tyrannosaurus Rex

by Susan Jones Leeming

PEARSON
Scott
Foresman

DK

What You Already Know

Fossils are the remains of plants or animals that lived long ago. A fossil can look like an animal footprint or a print of a leaf. Some animal fossils come from old bones or other animal parts. They were made after an animal died and got covered by layers of mud. Over thousands of years the mud turned to stone. The shape of the animal got left in the stone.

Paleontologists study fossils to find out about animals that are extinct, or that are no longer living on Earth. Dinosaurs are extinct animals. Paleontologists study their fossil remains to learn about them. Through studying fossils, paleontologists get ideas about how dinosaurs looked and what they ate.

ammonite fossil

Paleontologists learn new things when they find new fossils. Not too long ago they made a new discovery about a dinosaur called Oviraptor. Paleontologists thought they had found a fossil of an Oviraptor stealing and eating eggs. Now they know the eggs were the Oviraptors' own.

In this book, you will read about some other dinosaur discoveries. You will learn what paleontologists have discovered about a dinosaur called Tyrannosaurus rex.

Tyrannosaurus rex

Who was T. rex?

Tyrannosaurus rex, or T. rex for short, is one of the most famous dinosaurs to walk the Earth. Tyrannosaurus rex is a Latin name. It means "tyrant king lizard."

T. rex is one of the largest meat-eating animals ever to have lived. It could grow as long as a large fire truck and as heavy as three cars. T. rex was tall enough to see over the top of an elephant!

During the Cretaceous period Earth looked very different than it looks today.

This giant lived at the end of the Cretaceous (kri-TAY-shuhs) period. This is what scientists call the time when dinosaurs such as T. rex lived. The Cretaceous period was the time between 135 million and 70 million years ago.

Scientists believe that Earth changed a lot during the Cretaceous period. The Earth's continents moved and changed shape. At the end of the Cretaceous period, dinosaurs became extinct.

T. rex was one of the biggest meat-eating dinosaurs of the Cretaceous period.

Discovery!

T. rex became extinct at the end of the Cretaceous period, but some T. rex bodies got buried under sand and mud. Their skeletons slowly turned into fossils.

Barnum Brown was one of the first scientists to study dinosaurs. In 1902 he found some fossils in Montana, U.S.A. It was hard to excavate the fossils, as they were buried in rock. The fossils turned out to be the bones of a T. rex skeleton!

After the scientists dug out the fossil bones, they moved them to a museum in New York. Scientists at the museum studied the fossils. They rebuilt the T. rex skeleton.

Barnum Brown, a scientist, discovered T. rex fossils in 1902.

T. rex skeleton

Scientists have found T. rex bones in other parts of North America. These discoveries have given us clues about where T. rex lived. The bones have also given scientists a way to study T. rex's anatomy. An animal's anatomy is how its body looks and works.

excavation of T. rex at Hell Creek, Montana

T. rex Anatomy

If you look at the anatomy of T. rex, you will see that its feet looked a little like bird feet. Each foot had three toes with claws.

T. rex's long, scaly back legs had very strong muscles. T. rex needed these muscles to support its heavy body. T. rex's forelegs were much smaller! They didn't even reach its mouth.

Scientists think T. rex used its small forelegs for balance. T. rex may have used them to get up off the ground after lying down.

T. rex's feet had three bird-like toes.

For some time scientists believed T. rex moved upright like a penguin. They thought its thick, heavy tail hung straight down, almost touching the ground. Now, scientists have computer animation models of T. rex. Scientists use these models to get new ideas about how T. rex might have moved.

Scientists now think that T. rex must have moved with its chest closer to the ground. It may have lifted its tail off the ground to help balance its heavy body.

T. rex probably ran with its chest to the ground, using its tail for balance.

Perhaps T. rex had holes in its skull to make it lighter.

T. rex had a very heavy skull. Fossil T. rex skulls have large and small holes. Some of these holes were for its eyes and ears. Scientists think that some of the holes were empty space to make the skull lighter.

When you see how large T. rex was, its brain seems tiny! But T. rex's brain was bigger than those of many plant-eating dinosaurs. This may be because T. rex needed to do more thinking. Instead of just eating plants, it needed to think about how to hunt and catch its prey.

T. rex had powerful jaws filled with saw-like teeth.

T. rex had very powerful jaws. A T. rex could have swallowed a human being whole! Its teeth had saw-like edges. These teeth left marks in the bones of the animals it ate. Scientists can use these bones to figure out what T. rex ate.

Each T. rex tooth was at least seven inches long. This is about as long as your forearm! With jaws and teeth like that, T. rex could easily eat other animals.

fossil of a T. rex tooth

Hunter or scavenger?

A hunter is an animal that eats other animals it catches. A scavenger is an animal that eats the leftover parts of animals caught by others.

Many scientists think T. rex was mostly a hunter. They think that T. rex used its strong back legs to chase other animals. They think it killed its prey with its powerful jaws. Animals that hunt need to have good eyes. Some scientists think that T. rex could see very well.

T. rex used its powerful jaws to eat its kill. But did it hunt for its food or scavenge?

Other scientists think that T. rex was a scavenger. They think its eyes were too small to see well. They think T. rex was too heavy to run fast. These scientists also think that T. rex used a large part of its brain for smelling. Scavengers need to be able to smell dead animals from very far away.

In truth, T. rex was probably both a hunter and a scavenger. It used its eyes and powerful jaws to hunt and kill smaller animals. It may also have used its sense of smell to find dead dinosaurs to scavenge.

Although scientists may not agree on how T. rex ate, they do agree on what it ate. Fossils of dinosaur dung show that T. rex ate mostly smaller, plant-eating dinosaurs. It also may have eaten a large dinosaur called Triceratops. Triceratops was a plant eater, but it had sharp horns and thick skin. Triceratops must have been hard to catch and eat, even for T. rex with its powerful jaws!

T. rex probably ate slow-moving duck-billed dinosaurs.

Dinosaur Mysteries

T. rex is one of the most interesting and amazing animals that ever lived. Paleontologists still want to know more about this "king of lizards." Perhaps scientists will discover new fossils that will help us learn more. Perhaps they will find new ways to study fossils. Maybe we will find out for sure if T. rex was a hunter or a scavenger. Until then, many people will ask questions about this mysterious giant. What questions do you have?

Glossary

anatomy

how an animal's body looks and moves

computer animation models

computer images of how animals move

continents

seven great areas of land on Earth

Cretaceous period

the time when T. rex lived

dung

animal waste

excavate

to dig up and remove from the ground

scavenger

an animal that finds and eats leftover parts of dead animals

What did you learn?

1. What is the Cretaceous period?

2. Why did T. rex have a lot of holes in its skull?

3. **Writing** in Science Scientists changed their ideas about how T. rex moved. Write to explain what scientists used to think and what they think now. What made them change their minds?

4. **Retell** Some scientists think that T. rex was a hunter and some think he was a scavenger. In your own words tell what clues we have about how T. rex got its food. Use the information on pages 12–13 to help you.

Genre	Comprehension Skill	Text Features	Science Content
Nonfiction	Retell	• Captions • Labels • Glossary	Fossils and Dinosaurs

Scott Foresman Science 2.7

PEARSON

Scott Foresman

scottforesman.com

ISBN 0-328-13789-8

90000

9 780328 137893